DRYDEN'S KING ARTHUR

KING ARTHUR

OR

THE BRITISH WORTHY

A Dramatick Opera

BY

JOHN DRYDEN

As Performed at the New Theatre
Cambridge
14–18 February 1928
with
The Alterations Adopted
by
HENRY PURCELL

Cambridge
at the University Press
1928

CAMBRIDGE
UNIVERSITY PRESS

University Printing House, Cambridge CB2 8BS, United Kingdom

Cambridge University Press is part of the University of Cambridge.

It furthers the University's mission by disseminating knowledge in the pursuit of education, learning and research at the highest international levels of excellence.

www.cambridge.org
Information on this title: www.cambridge.org/9781107486881

© Cambridge University Press 1928

First published 1928
Re-issued 2015

A catalogue record for this publication is available from the British Library

ISBN 978-1-107-48688-1 Paperback

INTRODUCTION

I

On June the 3rd, 1685, *Albion and Albanius*, an allegorical opera by Dryden and Grabu, was produced. Originally intended to immortalise Charles II and the Duke of York, this work was altered after Charles's death to flatter the new king. Like the allegorical introductions to the foreign operas of the day, *Albion and Albanius* was to be an extended prologue to a great patriotic music drama, but at least two chances helped to damn the prologue and to postpone the writing of the opera proper. News reached London that the Duke of Monmouth had landed in the west, and—as Downes says—"The Nation being in a great consternation, it was performed but Six times, which not Answering half THE Charge they were at, Involv'd the Company very much in debt". Dryden was besides guilty of a serious error of judgment in choosing for his composer Charles II's French Master of Musick, who was by no means a rival to his fellow-countryman Lulli and who, though possibly a favourite of the king, was not admired by serious English musicians. Dryden's preface alludes slightingly to English composers and Grabu's dedication insults English singers. Small wonder then that there was no immediate prospect of the patriotic opera seeing the light.

By 1691 however William and Mary were firmly established and Purcell was generally recognised as a master composer. Dryden accordingly rose to the occasion and produced *King Arthur* as a grand patriotic opera in collaboration with the new genius.

To judge from the Epistle Dedicatory the collaboration was genuine. Dryden writes:

I have been oblig'd so much to alter the first Design...that it is now no more what it was formerly, than the present Ship of the *Royal Sovereign*, after so often taking down, and altering, to the Vessel it was at the first Building. There is nothing better, than what I intended, but the Musick; which has since arriv'd to a greater Perfection in *England*, than ever formerly; especially passing through the Artful Hands of Mr. *Purcel*, who has Compos'd it with so great a Genius, that he has nothing to fear but an ignorant, ill-judging Audience. But the Numbers of Poetry and Vocal Musick, are sometimes so contrary, that in many places I have been oblig'd to cramp my Verses, and make them rugged to the Reader, that they may be harmonious to the Hearer: Of which I have no Reason to repent me, because these sorts of Entertainment are principally design'd for the

Ear and Eye; and therefore in Reason my Art,
on this occasion, ought to be subservient to his.
And besides, I flatter my self with an Imagi-
nation, that a Judicious Audience will easily
distinguish betwixt the Songs, wherein I have
comply'd with him, and those in which I have
followed the Rules of Poetry, in the Sound and
Cadence of the Words.

King Arthur was first produced at the Dorset
Garden Theatre in December 1691 with the
following cast:

Arthur	...	Betterton
Oswald	...	Williams
Conon	...	Hodgson
Merlin	...	Kynaston
Osmond	...	Sandford
Aurelius	...	Alexander
Albanact	...	Bowen
Guillamar	...	Harris
Emmeline	...	Mrs Bracegirdle
Matilda	...	Mrs Richardson
Philidel	...	Mrs Butler
Grimbald	...	Mr Bowman

It was played several times[1] and seen by
the Queen and her Maids of Honour on
January 7, 1691/2[2].

[1] *Gentleman's Journal*, January 1692.
[2] Nicoll's *Restoration Drama*. Lord Chamberlain's
Records 5/151, p. 369.

The opera was revived in 1736, and in 1770 Garrick produced it with "some slight Alterations . . . for the greater Convenience of Representation" and some new songs by Arne, "where it was thought such Additions would be of Service to the whole". The cast on this occasion included Mrs Baddeley as Philidel and Vernon, a tenor who had earlier been famous as a male soprano.

It was again revived in 1781 "the first time for six years" with Miss Wright (Michael Arne's wife?) as the priestess and a siren. In 1784 Kemble played Arthur and still more music was added by Linley.

In the nineteenth century there were four revivals. In 1803 Mrs Siddons appeared as Emmeline, and her husband as Oswald: in 1819 it was staged at Covent Garden: in 1827 it was produced at the English Opera House without Arne's music but with additions from Purcell's *Indian Queen* and *Dido and Aeneas*, and, for the last time, under Macready's direction at Drury Lane in 1842 with twelve additional characters, a new masque, a quantity of interpolated music from Purcell's other dramatic works, and such a profusion of "sparkling of the waters in the sunlight, and the glittering spray as it descends a rocky eminence" that the audience applauded the production rather than the music, and Macready was severely criticised[1].

The present 1928 revival at Cambridge is therefore perhaps the first complete revival since the seventeenth century in the spirit and—as far as possible—in the manner intended by Dryden and Purcell.

II

By the autumn of 1690, though experienced as a composer, Henry Purcell, aged thirty-one[2], had barely begun to make his name as a writer for the theatre. He had to his credit —apart from a few songs, elegies, catches, the Sonatas in three parts, and the Service in B flat—twenty Odes or Welcome Songs and about fifty anthems. It is true that he had already written music for some sixteen plays, but the music in most of these consists merely of an occasional song or instrumental piece— with the exception of *Dido and Aeneas*, *The Tempest*(?) and *Dioclesian*.

There is nothing to show that the freak masterpiece *Dido and Aeneas* attracted any attention outside the friendly audience at the school where it was produced. But *Dioclesian* was so effective that Dryden allowed Purcell to set the songs in his *Amphitryon* and as a

[1] *Dramatic and Musical Review*, November 19, 1842.
[2] See *Henry Purcell* (Oxford Press), by the present writer.

result was moved to write in the prefatory letter

what has been wanting on my Part, has been abundantly supplyed by the Excellent Composition of Mr. *Purcell*; in whose Person we have at length found an *English-Man*, equal with the best abroad. At least my Opinion of him has been such, since his happy and judicious Performances in the late *Opera*; and the Experience I have had of him, in the setting my three Songs for this *Amphitryon*. To all of which, and particularly to the Composition of the *Pastoral Dialogue*, the numerous Quire of Fair Ladies gave so just an Applause on the Third Day.

The result was *King Arthur* and the music to thirty-seven other plays in the last five years of Purcell's life.

Unfortunately the original score was soon lost—possibly with the *Fairy Queen* music as early as 1701. Two hundred years later the latter was discovered in the Library of the Royal Academy of Music, but the whereabouts of the original *King Arthur* manuscript is still unknown.

For this revival and for the Purcell Society Edition I have consulted the following MSS.:

A MS. at the Royal Academy of Music (dated 1698/9).

A MS. at Oriel College (late seventeenth or early eighteenth century).

Four early eighteenth century MSS. at Tenbury, the British Museum and the Fitzwilliam Museum.

Seven late eighteenth century MSS. at the British Museum, the Royal Music Library, Gresham College, the Royal College of Music and the library of the late W. H. Cummings.

Fourteen fragmentary MSS. dating from c. 1704 to c. 1798.

None of these, however, are complete and none accurate[1].

Apart from editions of the whole opera—Taylor's and Macfarren's (1843), Arkwright's (1889), Cummings's (1897), and Fuller Maitland's (1897)—various numbers have been printed from 1696 to the present day, the most popular being "Come, if you dare", "Fairest Isle" and portions of the "Frost Scene": not to mention a Dramatic Fantasia on the latter (1842), "The King Arthur Quadrilles" (1843) and "The Rifleman's March" introducing "Come, if you dare" (1860).

The music was scored for two flutes, two hautboys, two trumpets, drums[2], strings and *continuo*.

DENNIS ARUNDELL

[1] With regard to the numbers marked in the text as missing, it is quite probable that these were never set by Purcell so as to avoid holding up the action.

[2] No drum parts have survived, but they were obviously used.

℈ The text has been taken from the first collected edition of 1701, obvious errors being corrected.

℈ Lines enclosed in square brackets [ ] were omitted in the 1928 production.

PROLOGUE TO THE OPERA

Spoken by Mr Betterton

SUre there's a Dearth of Wit in this dull Town,
When silly Plays so savourly go down:
As when Clipp'd Money passes, 'tis a sign
A Nation is not over-stock'd with Coin.
Happy is he, who, in his own Defence,
Can Write just level to your humble Sence;
Who higher than your Pitch can never go;
And doubtless, he must creep, who Writes below.
So have I seen in Hall of Knight, or Lord,
A weak Arm, throw on a long Shovel-Board,
He barely lays his Piece, bar Rubs and Knocks,
Secur'd by weakness not to reach the Box.
A Feeble Poet will his Bus'ness do;
Who straining all he can, comes up to you:
For if you like your Selves, you like him too.
An Ape his own Dear Image will embrace;
An ugly Beau adores a Hatchet Face:
So some of you, on pure instinct of Nature,
Are led, by Kind, t' admire your fellow Creature.
In fear of which, our House has sent this Day,
T' insure our New-Built-Vessel, call'd a Play.
No sooner Nam'd than one crys out, These Stagers
Come in good time, to make more Work for Wagers.
The Town divides, if it will take, or no, ⎫
The Courtiers Bet, the Cits, the Merchants too; ⎬
A sign they have but little else to do. ⎭

Betts, at the firſt, were Fool-Traps; where the Wiſe
Like Spiders, lay in Ambuſh for the Flies:
But now they're grown a common Trade for all,
And Actions, by the News-Book, Riſe and Fall.
Wits, Cheats, and Fops, are free of Wager-Hall.
One Policy, as far as Lyons *carries;*
Another, nearer home ſets up for Paris.
Our Betts, at laſt, wou'd ev'n to Rome *extend,*
But that the Pope has prov'd our Truſty Friend.
Indeed, it were a Bargain, worth our Money,
Cou'd we inſure another Ottobuoni.
Among the reſt, there are a sharping Sett,
That Pray for us, and yet againſt us Bett:
Sure Heav'n it ſelf, is at a loſs to know,
If theſe wou'd have their Pray'rs be heard, or no:
For in great Stakes, we piously ſuppoſe,
Men Pray but very faintly they may loſe.
Leave off theſe Wagers; for in Conſcience Speaking,
The City needs not your new Tricks for breaking:
And if you Gallants loſe, to all appearing
You'll want an Equipage for Volunteering;
While thus, no Spark of Honour left within ye,
When you shou'd draw the Sword, you draw the Guinea.]

DRAMATIS PERSONAE

King *Arthur*.
Ofwald, King of *Kent*, a Saxon and a Heathen.
Conon, Duke of *Cornwal*, Tributary to King
  Arthur.
Merlin, a famous *Inchanter*.
Ofmond, a Saxon Magician, and a Heathen.
Aurelius, Friend to *Arthur*.
Albanaƈt, Captain of *Arthur*'s Guards.
Guillamar, Friend to *Ofwald*.

Emmeline, Daughter of *Conon*.
Matilda, her Attendant.

Philidel, an Airy Spirit.
Grimbald, an Earthy Spirit.

Officers and Soldiers, Singers and Dancers, *&c.*

Scene in *KENT*.

KING ARTHUR

OR

THE BRITISH WORTHY

Enter Conon, Aurelius, Albanact.

Con. Then this is the deciding Day, to fix
Great Britain's Scepter in great *Arthur's* Hand.
Aur. Or put it in the bold Invaders gripe.
Arthur and *Oswald*, and their different Fates,
Are weighing now within the Scales of
    Heaven.
Con. In Ten set Battels have we driven back
These Heathen Saxons, and regain'd our
    Earth.
As Earth recovers from an Ebbing Tide,
Her half-drown'd Face, and lifts it o'er the
    Waves.
From *Severn's* Banks, even to this *Barren-Down*,
Our foremost Men have prest their fainty
    Rear,
And not one Saxon Face has been beheld;
But all their Backs, and Shoulders have
    been stuck

I

With foul dishoneſt Wounds: Now here,
    indeed,
Becauſe they have no further Ground they
    ſtand.
  Aur. Well have we choſe a Happy day,
    for Fight;
For every Man, in courſe of time, has
    found
Some days are lucky, ſome unfortunate.
  Alb. But why this day more lucky than
    the reſt?
  Con. Becauſe this day
Is Sacred to the Patron of our Isle;
A Chriſtian, and a Souldier's Annual Feaſt.
  Alb. Oh, now I underſtand you, This is
    St. *George* of *Cappadocia*'s Day.
Well, it may be ſo, but Faith I was Ignorant;
    we Souldiers
Seldom examine the Rubrick; and now and
    then a Saint may
Happen to slip by us; But if he be a Gentle-
    man Saint, he will
Forgive us.
  Con. *Oſwald*, undoubtedly, will Fight it
    bravely.
  Aur. And it behoves him well, 'tis his
    laſt Stake.   [*To* Alb.
But what manner of Man is this *Oſwald*?
    Have ye ever ſeen him?

Alb. Ne'er but once; and that was to my
    Coſt too; I follow'd him too cloſe;
And to ſay Truth, ſomewhat Uncivilly,
    upon a Rout;
But he turn'd upon me, as quick and as
    round, as a chaf'd Boar;
And gave me two Licks acroſs the Face,
    to put me
In mind of my Chriſtianity.
  Con. I know him well; he's free and open
    Hearted.
  Aur. His Countries Character: That Speaks
    a German.
  Con. Revengeful, rugged, violently brave;
    and once reſolv'd, is never to be
    mov'd.
  Alb. Yes, he's a valiant Dog, Pox on him.
  Con. This was the Character he then
    maintain'd,
When in my Court he ſought my Daughter's
    Love:
My Fair, Blind, *Emmeline.*
  Alb. I cannot blame him for Courting the
    Heireſs of *Cornwal*:
All Heireſſes are Beautiful; and as Blind as
    she is, he would have had
No Blind Bargain of her.
  Aur. For that Defeat in Love, he rais'd
    this War.

For Royal *Arthur* Reign'd within her Heart,
E'er *Ofwald* mov'd his Sute.

  Con. Ay, now *Aurelius*, you have Nam'd
    a Man;
One, whom befides the Homage that I owe,
As *Cornwal*'s Duke, to his Imperial Crown,
I wou'd have chofen out, from all Mankind,
To be my Soveraign Lord.

  Aur. His worth divides him from the croud
    of Kings;
So Born, without Defert to be fo Born;
Men, fet aloft, to be the Scourge of Heaven;
And with long Arms, to lash the Under-
    World.

  Con. Arthur is all that's Excellent in *Ofwald*;
And void of all his Faults: In Battel brave;
But ftill Serene in all the Stormy War,
Like Heaven above the Clouds; and after
    Fight,
As Merciful and Kind, to vanquisht Foes,
As a forgiving God; but fee, he's here,
And Praife is Dumb before him.

     Enter King Arthur, *Reading a Letter,*
       with Attendants.

  Arthur ⎱Go on, Aufpicious Prince, the
  Reading.⎰   Stars are kind:
Unfold thy Banners to the willing Wind;
While I, with Airy Legions, help thy Arms:

Confronting Art with Art, and Charms
    with Charms.
So *Merlin* writes; nor can we doubt
    th' event,   [*To* Con.
With Heav'n and you to Friends; Oh Noble
    Conon,
You taught my tender Hands the Trade of
    War;
And now again you Helm your Hoary Head,
And under double weight of Age and Arms,
Affert your Country's Freedom, and my
    Crown.
  Con. No more, my Son.
  Arth. Moft happy in that Name!
Your *Emmeline*, to *Ofwald*'s Vows refus'd,
You made my plighted Bride:
Your Charming Daughter, who like Love,
    Born Blind,
Un-aiming hits, with fureft Archery,
And Innocently kills.
  Con. Remember, Son,
You are a General, other Wars require you.
For fee the *Saxon* Grofs begins to move.
  Arth. Their Infantry Embattel'd, fquare
    and clofe,
March firmly on, to fill the middle fpace:
Cover'd by their advancing Cavalry.
By Heav'n, 'tis Beauteous Horrour:
The Noble *Ofwald* has provok'd my Envy.

Enter Emmeline, *led by* Matilda.

Ha! Now my Beauteous *Emmeline* appears,
Anew, but Oh, a fofter Flame, infpires me:
Even Rage and Vengeance, slumber at
    her fight.

  Con. Hafte your Farewel; I'll chear my
    Troops, and wait ye.   [*Exit* Conon.
  Em. Oh Father, Father, I am fure you're
    here;
Becaufe I fee your Voice.
  Arth. No, thou miftak'ft thy hearing for
    thy fight;
He's gone, my *Emmeline*;
And I but ftay to gaze on thofe fair Eyes,
Which cannot view the Conqueft they
    have made.
Oh Star-like Night, dark only to thy felf,
But full of Glory, as thofe Lamps of Heav'n
That fee not when they shine.
  Em. What is this Heav'n, and Stars, and
    Night, and Day,
To which you thus compare my Eyes and me?
I underftand you, when you fay you love:
For, when my Father clafps my Hand in his,
That's cold, and I can feel it hard and
    wrinckl'd;
But when you grafp it, then I figh and pant,
And fomething fmarts, and tickles at my
    Heart.

  Arth. Oh Artlefs Love! where the Soul
     moves the Tongue,
And only Nature fpeaks what Nature thinks!
Had she but Eyes!
  Em. Juft now you faid I had:
I fee 'em, I have two.
  Arth. But neither fee.
  Em. I'm fure they hear you then:
What can your Eyes do more?
  [*Arth.* They view your Beauties.
  Em. Do not I fee You have a Face like
     mine,
Two Hands, and two round, pretty, rifing
     Breafts,
That heave like mine.
  Arth. But you defcribe a Woman.
Nor is it fight, but touching with your Hands.
  Em. Then 'tis my Hand that fees, and that's
     all one:
For is not feeing, touching with your Eyes?
  Arth. No, for I fee at diftance, where I
     touch not.
  Em. If you can fee fo far, and yet not touch,
I fear you fee my Naked Legs and Feet
Quite through my Cloaths; pray do not fee
     fo well.
  Arth. Fear not, fweet Innocence;]
I view the lovely Features of your Face;
Your Lips Carnation, your dark shaded
     Eye-brows,

Black Eyes, and Snow-white Forehead; all
    the Colours
That make your Beauty, and produce my Love.
  Em. Nay, then, you do not love on equal
    terms:
I love you dearly, without all thefe helps:
I cannot fee your Lips Carnation,
Your shaded Eye-brows, nor your Milk-
    white Eyes.
  Arth. You ftill miftake.
  Em. Indeed I thought you had a Nofe
    and Eyes,
And fuch a Face as mine; have not Men Faces?
  Arth. Oh, none like yours, fo excellently fair.
  Em. Then wou'd I had no Face; for I
    wou'd be
Juft fuch a one as you.
  Arth. Alas, 'tis vain to inftruct your
    Innocence,
You have no Notion of Light or Colours.
               [*Trumpet founds within.*
  Em. Why, is not that a Trumpet?
  Arth. Yes.
  Em. I knew it.
And I can tell you how the found on't looks.
It looks as if it had an angry fighting Face.
  Arth. 'Tis now indeed a sharp unpleafant
    found,
Becaufe it calls me hence, from her I love,

To meet Ten thoufand Foes.

 Em. How does fo many Men e'er come
  to meet?
This Devil Trumpet vexes 'em, and then
They feel about, for one anothers Faces;
And fo they meet, and kill.

 Arth. I'll tell ye all, when we have gain'd
  the Field;
One kifs of your fair Hand, the pledge of
  Conqueft,
And fo a short farewel.

     [*Kiffes her Hand, and* Exit *with
        Aurel. Alb. *and Attendants.*

 Em. My Heart, and Vows, go with him to
  the Fight:
May every Foe be that, which they call blind,
And none of all their Swords have Eyes to
  find him.
But lead me nearer to the Trumpet's Face;
For that brave Sound upholds my fainting
  Heart;
And while I hear, methinks I fight my part.
       [*Exit, led by* Matilda.

   Enter Ofwald *and* Ofmond.

*The Scene reprefents a place of Heathen Worship;
 The three Saxon Gods*, Woden, Thor, *and*
 Freya *placed on Pedeftals. An Altar.*

 Ofmo. 'Tis time to haften our myfterious Rites;

           2

Becaufe your Army waits you.

> [Ofwald *making three Bows before
> the three Images.*

Ofwa. *Thor, Freya, Woden,* all ye Saxon
> Powers,

Hear and revenge my Father *Hengift*'s Death.

Ofmo. Father of Gods and Men, great
> *Woden,* hear.

Mount thy hot Courfer, drive amidft thy Foes;

Lift high thy thund'ring Arm, let every blow

Dash out a mif-believing Briton's Brains.

Ofwa. Father of Gods and Men, great
> *Woden* hear;

Give Conqueft to thy Saxon Race, and me.

Ofmo. *Thor, Freya, Woden,* hear, and fpell
> your Saxons,

With Sacred Runick Rhimes, from Death
> in Battel.

Edge their bright Swords, and blunt the
> Britons Darts.

No more, Great Prince, for fee my trufty Fiend,

Who all the Night has wing'd the dusky Air.

> [Grimbald, *a fierce earthy Spirit arifes.*

What News, my *Grimbald*?

Grim. I have plaid my part;

For I have Steel'd the Fools that are to die;

Six Fools, fo prodigal of Life and Soul,

That, for their Country, they devote their
> Lives

A Sacrifice to Mother Earth, and *Woden*.

Ofmo. 'Tis well; But are we fure of
    Victory?

Grim. Why ask'ft thou me?

Infpect their Intrails, draw from thence
    thy Guefs:

Bloud we muft have, without it we are
    dumb.

Ofmo. Say, Where's thy Fellow-fervant,
    Philidel?

Why comes not he?

Grim. For, he's a puleing Sprite.

Why didft thou chufe a tender airy Form,

Unequal to the mighty work of Mifchief;

His Make is flitting, foft, and yielding
    Atomes:

He trembles at the yawning gulph of Hell,

Nor dares approach the Flame, left he
    should finge

His gaudy filken Wings.

He fighs when he should plunge a Soul in
    Sulphur,

As with Compaffion, touch'd of foolish Man.

Ofmo. What a half Devil's he?

His errand was, to draw the Low-land damps,

And Noifom Vapours, from the foggy Fens:

Then, breath the baleful ftench, with all his
    force,

Full on the faces of our Chriftned Foes.

Grim. Accordingly he drein'd thofe
    Marshy grounds;
And bagg'd 'em in a blue Peftiferous Cloud;
Which when he shou'd have blown, the
    frighted Elf
Efpy'd the Red Crofs Banners of their Hoft;
And faid he durft not add to his damnation.
  Ofmo. I'll punish him at leifure;
Call in the Victims to propitiate Hell.
  Grim. That's my kind Mafter, I shall break
    faft on 'em.

[Grimbald *goes to the Door, and Re-enters with
    fix Saxons in White, with Swords in their hands.
    They range themfelves three and three in Oppo-
    fition to each other.*

The reft of the Stage is fill'd with Priefts and Singers.

Woden, *firft to thee,*
A Milk-white Steed in Battel won,
We have Sacrific'd.
  Chor. *We have Sacrific'd.*
  Verf. *Let our next oblation be,*
To Thor, *thy thundring Son,*
Of fuch another.
  Chor. *We have Sacrific'd.*
  Verf. *A Third; (of* Friezland *breed was he,)*
To Woden's *Wife, and to* Thor's *Mother:*
And now we have atton'd all three
We have Sacrific'd.
  Chor. *We have Sacrific'd.*

2 Voc. *The White Horſe Neigh'd aloud.*
To Woden *thanks we render.*
To Woden, *we have vow'd.*
  Chor. *To* Woden, *our Defender.*
            [The four laſt Lines in *CHORUS*.
  Verſ. *The Lot is caſt, and* Tanfan *pleas'd:*
  Chor. *Of Mortal Cares you shall be eas'd,*
**Brave Souls to be renown'd in Story.*
Honour prizing,
Death deſpiſing,
Fame acquiring
By Expiring,
Die, and reap the fruit of Glory.
Brave Souls to be renown'd in Story.
  Verſ. 2. †*I call ye all,*
To Woden*'s Hall;*
Your Temples round
With Ivy bound,
In Goblets Crown'd,
And plenteous Bowls of burnish'd Gold;
Where you shall Laugh,
And dance and quaff,
The Juice, that makes the Britons bold.†
            [*The ſix Saxons are led off by the Prieſts,*
                        in Order to be Sacrific'd.
  Oſw. Ambitious Fools we are,
And yet ambition is a Godlike Fault:
Or rather, 'tis no Fault in Souls born great,

    * In Purcell's setting the chorus begins here.
    † Repeated as a chorus.

Who dare extend their Glory by their Deeds.
Now *Britany* prepare to change thy State,
And from this Day begin thy Saxon date.

> [*Exeunt Omnes.*

A Battel fuppofed to be given behind the
Scenes, with Drums, Trumpets, and Military
Shouts and Excurfions: After which, the
Britons, expreffing their Joy for the Victory,
fing this Song of Triumph.*

Come if you dare, our Trumpets found;
Come if you dare, the Foes rebound:
We come, we come, we come, we come,
Says the double, double, double Beat of the
  Thundring Drum.
  Now they charge on amain,
  Now they rally again:
The Gods from above the mad Labour behold,
And pity Mankind that will perish for Gold.
The Fainting Saxons *quit their Ground,*
Their Trumpets Languish in the Sound;
They fly, they fly, they fly, they fly;
Victoria, Victoria, *the Bold* Britons *cry.*
  Now the Victory's won,
  To the Plunder we run:
We return to our Laffes like Fortunate Traders,
Triumphant with Spoils of the Vanquisht Invaders.

* Purcell inserts a military symphony between the
verses of the song.

ACT II.

Enter Philidel.

Phil. Alas, for pity, of this bloody Field!
Piteous it needs muſt be, when I, a Spirit,
Can have ſo ſoft a ſenſe of Humane Woes!
Ah! for ſo many Souls, as but this Morn,
Were cloath'd with Flesh, and warm'd with
    Vital blood,
But naked now, or shirted but with Air.
     [Merlin, *with Spirits, deſcends to* Philidel,
         on a Chariot drawn by Dragons.
  Mer. What art thou, Spirit, of what Name
    and Order?
(For I have view'd thee in my Magick
    Glaſs,)
Making thy moan, among the Midnight
    Wolves,
That Bay the ſilent Moon: Speak, I Conjure
    thee.
'Tis *Merlin* bids thee, at whoſe awful Wand,
The pale Ghoſt quivers, and the grim Fiend
    gaſps.
  Phil. An Airy Shape, the tender'ſt of my
    kind,
The laſt ſeduc'd, and leaſt deform'd of Hell;
Half white, and shuffl'd in the Crowd, I fell;
Deſirous to repent, and loth to ſin;

Awkward in Mifchief, piteous of Mankind,
My Name is *Philidel*, my Lot in Air;
Where next beneath the Moon, and nearest
    Heav'n,
I foar, and have a Glimpfe to be receiv'd,
For which the fwarthy *Dæmons* envy me.
  Mer. Thy Bufinefs here?
  Phil. To fhun the Saxon Wizards dire
    Commands,
Ofmond, the awful'ft Name next thine below,
'Caufe I refus'd to hurl a Noyfom Fog
On Chriften'd Heads, the Hue and Cry of
    Hell
Is rais'd againft me, for a Fugitive Spright.
  Mer. *Ofmond* fhall know, a greater Power
    protects thee;
But follow thou the Whifpers of thy Soul,
That draw thee nearer Heav'n.
And, as thy Place is nearest to the Sky,
The Rays will reach thee firft, and bleach
    thy Soot.
  Phil. In hope of that, I fpread my Azure
    Wings,
And wifhing ftill, for yet I dare not pray,
I bafk in Day-light, and behold with Joy
My Scum work outward, and my Ruft
    wear off.
  Mer. Why 'tis my hopeful Devil; now mark
    me, *Philidel*,

I will employ thee, for thy future Good:
Thou know'ſt, in ſpite of Valiant *Oſwald*'s
    Arms,
Or *Oſmond*'s Powerful Spells, the Field is
    ours. ──

 Phil. Oh, Maſter! haſten
Thy Dread Commands, for *Grimbald* is at
    Hand;
Oſmond's fierce Fiend, I ſnuff his Earthly
    Scent:
The Conquering *Britons*, he misleads to
    Rivers,
Or dreadful Downfals of unheeded Rocks;
Where many fall, that ne'er shall riſe
    again.

 Mer. Be that thy care, to ſtand by falls
    of Brooks,
And trembling Bogs, that bear a Green-
    Sword show.
Warn off the bold Purſuers from the Chace:
No more, they come, and we divide the
    Task.
But leſt fierce *Grimbald*'s pond'rous Bulk
    oppreſs
Thy tender flitting Air, I'll leave my Band
Of Spirits with United ſtrength to Aid thee,
And force with force repel.

        [*Exit* Merlin *on his Chariot.* Merlin'*s*
                Spirits ſtay with Philidel.

Enter Grimbald *in the Habit of a Shepherd,*
     follow'd by King Arthur, Conon, Aurelius,
     Albanact *and Souldiers, who wander at a*
     diſtance in the Scenes.

  Grim. Here, this way, *Britons,* follow *Oſwald*'s
     flight;
This Evening as I whiſtl'd out my Dog,
To drive my ſtraggling Flock, and pitch'd my
     Fold,
I ſaw him dropping Sweat, o'er-labour'd, ſtiff,
Make faintly as he could, to yonder Dell.
Tread in my Steps; long Neighbourhood
     by Day
Has made theſe Fields familiar in the Night.
  Arth. I thank thee, Shepherd;
Expect Reward, lead on, we follow thee.
  Phil. Sings.   *Hither this way, this way bend,*
                 Truſt not that Malicious Fiend:
                 Thoſe are falſe deluding Lights,
                 Wafted far and near by Sprights.
                 Truſt 'em not, for they'll deceive ye;
                 And in Bogs and Marshes leave ye.
  Chor. of Phil. Spirits. *Hither this way, this*
     way bend.
  Chor. of Grim. Spirits. *This way, this way bend.*
  Phil. Sings.   *If you ſtep, no Danger thinking,*
                 Down you fall, a Furlong ſinking:
                 'Tis a Fiend who has annoy'd ye;
                 Name but Heav'n, and he'll avoid ye.

Chor. of Phil. Spirits. *Hither this way, this way bend.*

Chor. of Grimb. Spirits. *This way, this way bend.*

Philidel's Spirits. *Truſt not that Malicious Fiend.*

Grimbald's Spirits. *Truſt me, I am no Malicious Fiend.**

Philidel's Spirits. *Hither this way,* &c.

Con. Some wicked Phantom, Foe to Human kind,

Miſguides our Steps.

Alb. I'll follow him no farther.

Grimbald ſpeaks. By Hell, he ſings 'em back, in my deſpight.

I had a voice in Heav'n, e're Sulph'rous Steams
Had damp'd it to a hoarſeneſs; but I'll try.

He ſings.   *Let not a Moon-born Elf mislead ye,*
From your Prey, and from your Glory.
Too far, Alas, he has betray'd ye:
Follow the Flames, that wave before ye:
Sometimes Seven, and ſometimes one;
Hurry, hurry, hurry, hurry on.

2.

See, ſee, the Footſteps plain appearing,
That way Oſwald *choſe for flying:*
Firm is the Turff, and fit for bearing,
Where yonder Pearly Dews are lying.
Far he cannot hence be gone;
Hurry, hurry, hurry, hurry on.

* This line omitted by Purcell.

Aur. 'Tis true, he fays; the Footfteps yet
    are fresh
Upon the Sod, no falling Dew-drops have
Difturb'd the Print.
        [*All are going to follow* Grimbald.
Philidel fings. *Hither this way.*
  Chor. of Phil. Spirits. *Hither this way, this*
    way bend.
  Chor. of Grimb. Spirits *This way, this way*
    bend.
  Philidel's Spirits. *Truft not that Malicious Fiend.*
  Grimb. Spirits. *Truft me, I am no Malicious*
    *Fiend.**
  Philidel's Spirits. *Hither this way,* &c.
        [*They all incline to* Philidel.
Grim. speaks. Curfe on her Voice, I muft my
    Prey forego;
Thou, *Philidel*, shall anfwer this below.
        [Grimbald *finks with a flash.*
Arth. At laft the Cheat is plain;
The Cloven-footed Fiend is Vanish'd from us;
Good Angels be our Guides, and bring us back.
  Phil. finging. †*Come follow, follow, follow me.*†
  Chor. *Come follow,* &c.
    And me. And me. And me. And me.
  Verfe. 2 Voc. *And Green-Sword all your way*
    shall be.

        * This line omitted by Purcell.
        † Set by Purcell as a quintet.

Chor. *Come follow*, &c.
Verſe. *No* Goblin *or* Elf *shall dare to offend ye.*
Chor. *No, no, no,* &c.
   No Goblin *or* Elf *shall dare to offend ye.*
Verſ. 3 Voc. *We Brethren of Air,*
   You Hero's *will bear,*
      To the Kind and the Fair that attend ye.
Chor. *We Brethren,* &c.

[Philidel *and the Spirits go off Singing, with King*
   Arthur *and the reſt in the middle of them. Enter*
   Emmeline *led by* Matilda. *Pavilion Scene.*

Em. No News of my Dear Love, or of my
      Father?
Mat. None, Madam, ſince the gaining of
      the Battel?
Great *Arthur* is a Royal Conqueror now
And well deſerves your Love.
Em. But now I fear
He'll be too great, to love poor ſilly me.
If he be dead, or never come agen,
I mean to die: But there's a greater doubt,
Since I ne'er ſaw him here,
How shall I meet him in another World?
Mat. I have heard ſomething, how two
      Bodies meet,
But how Souls joyn, I know not.
Em. I shou'd find him,
For ſurely I have ſeen him in my Sleep,

And then, methought, he put his Mouth
    to mine,
And eat a thoufand Kiffes on my Lips;
Sure by his Kiffing I cou'd find him out
Among a thoufand Angels in the Sky.
  Mat. But what a kind of Man do you
    fuppofe him?
  Em. He muft be made of the moft precious
    things:
And I believe his Mouth, and Eyes, and
    Cheeks,
And Nofe, and all his Face, are made of
    Gold.
  Mat. Heav'n blefs us, Madam, what a Face
    you make him!
If it be yellow, he muft have the Jaundies,
And that's a bad Difeafe.
  Em. Why then do Lovers give a thing fo bad
As Gold, to Women, whom fo well they Love?
  Mat. Becaufe that bad thing, Gold, buys all
    good things.
  Em. Yet I muft know him better: Of all
    Colours,
Tell me which is the pureft, and the fofteft.
  Mat. They fay 'tis Black.
  Em. Why then, fince Gold is hard, and yet
    is precious,
His Face muft all be made of foft, black Gold.
  Mat. But, Madam ——

Em. No more; I have learn'd enough for once.
Mat. Here are a Crew of Kentish Lads and
    Laſſes,
Wou'd entertain ye, till your Lord's return,
With Songs and Dances, to divert your Cares.
Em. O bring them in,
For tho' I cannot ſee the Songs, I love 'em;
And Love, they tell me, is a Dance of Hearts.

    Enter Shepherds and Shepherdeſſes.

1 Shep- ⎱ *How bleſt are Shepherds, how happy*
herd   ⎰   *their Laſſes,*
ſings.   ⎰ *While Drums and trumpets are*
           ſounding Alarms!
        Over our Lowly Sheds all the
           Storm paſſes;
        And when we die, 'tis in each
           others Arms.
        All the Day on our Heards and Flocks
           employing;
        All the Night on our Flutes, and in
           enjoying.
Chor.*   *All the Day,* &c.

        2.

        Bright Nymphs of Britain, *with*
           Graces attended,
        Let not your Days without Pleaſure
           expire;

  * Purcell repeats each verse in chorus.

Honour's but empty, and when Youth
  is ended,
All Men will praise you, but none
  will desire.
Let not Youth fly away without
  Contenting;
Age will come time enough, for your
  Repenting.

Chor. *Let not Youth, &c.*

[Here the Men offer their Flutes to the
  Women, which they refuse.

2 Shep-⎱ **Shepherd, Shepherd, leave Decoying,*
herdefs.⎰ *Pipes are sweet, a Summers Day;*
  But a little after Toying,
  Women have the shot to pay.

2.

Here are Marriage-Vows for signing,
  Set their Marks that cannot write:
After that, without Repining,
  Play and Welcome, Day and Night.

[Here the Women give the Men Con-
  tracts, which they accept.

Chor.⎱ *Come, Shepherds, lead up a lively*
of all.⎰ *Measure;*
  The Cares of Wedlock, are Cares
  of Pleasure:

  * Originally sung by two boys.

But whether Marriage bring Joy,
or Sorrow,
Make sure of this Day, and hang
to morrow.
[*The Dance after the Song, and* Exeunt
Shepherds and Shepherdesses.

Enter on the other side of the Stage, Oswald
and Guillamar.

Osw. The Night has wilder'd us; and we
are faln
Among their foremost Tents.
Guill. Ha! What are these!
They seem of more than Vulgar Quality.
Em. What Sounds are those? They cannot
far be distant:
Where are we now, *Matilda*?
Mat. Just before your Tent:
Fear not, they must be Friends, and they
approach.
Em. My *Arthur*, speak, my Love; Are you
return'd
To bless your *Emmeline*?
Oswa. to Guilla. I know that Face:
'Tis my Ungrateful Fair, who, scorning
mine,
Accepts my Rivals Love: Heav'n, thou'rt
bounteous,
Thou ow'st me nothing now.

4

Mat. Fear grows upon me:
Speak what you are; ſpeak, or I call for help.
  Oſwa. We are your Guards.
  Mat. Ah me! We are betray'd; 'tis
    Oſwald's Voice.
  Em. Let 'em not ſee our Voices, and then
    they cannot find us.
  Oſwa. Paſſions in Men Oppreſs'd are doubly
    ſtrong.
I take her from King *Arthur*; there's Revenge:
If she can love, she buoys my ſinking
    Fortunes:
Good Reaſons both: I'll on. —— Fear
    nothing, Ladies,
You shall be ſafe. [*Oſwald and Guillamar ſeize
               Emmeline and Matilda.*
  Em. & Matil. Help, help; a Rape, a Rape!
  Oſwa. By Heav'n ye injure me, thô Force
    is us'd,
Your Honour shall be ſacred.
  Em. Help, help, Oh *Britons* help!
  Oſwa. Your *Britons* cannot help you:
This Arm, through all their Troops, shall
    force my way;
Yet neither quit my Honour, nor my Prey.
        [*Exeunt, the Women ſtill crying.*

*An Alarm within: Some Soldiers running over the
    Stage: Follow, follow, follow.*

Enter Albanact *Captain of the Guards,*
with Soldiers.

Alb. Which way went th' Alarm?

1 *Sol.* Here, towards the Caſtle.

Alb. Pox o' this Victory; the whole Camp's
debauch'd:

All Drunk or Whoring: This way, follow,
follow.   [*Exeunt.*
> [*The Alarm renews: Clashing of Swords*
> *within for a while.*

Re-enter Albanact, *Officer and Soldiers.*

Officer. How ſits the Conqueſt on great
Arthur's Brow?

Alb. As when the Lover, with the King
is mixt,

He puts the gain of *Britain* in a Scale,

Which weighing with the loſs of *Emmeline*,

He thinks he's ſcarce a Saver.   [*Trumpet*

Officer. Hark! a Trumpet!   *within.*

It ſounds a Parley.

Alb. 'Tis from *Oſwald* then;

An Echo to King *Arthur*'s Friendly Summons,

Sent ſince he heard the Rape of *Emmeline*,

To ask an Interview.

> [*Trumpet anſwering on the other ſide.*

Officer. But hark! already

Our Trumpet makes reply; and ſee both
preſent.

Enter Arthur *on one fide attended,* Ofwald *on the other with Attendants, and* Guillamar. *They meet and falute.*

Arthur. Brave *Ofwald*! We have met on Friendlier Terms,
Companions of a War, with Common Intereft
Againft the Bordering *Picts*: But Times are chang'd.

Ofwa. And I am forry that thofe Times are chang'd:
For elfe we now might meet, on Terms as Friendly.

Arth. If fo we meet not now, the fault's your own;
For you have wrong'd me much.

Ofwa. Oh you wou'd tell me,
I call'd more *Saxons* in, t' enlarge my Bounds:
If thofe be Wrongs, the War has well redrefs'd ye.

Arth. Miftake me not, I count not War a Wrong:
War is the Trade of Kings, that fight for *Empire*;
And better be a Lyon, than a Sheep.

Ofwa. In what, then, have I wrong'd ye?

Arth. In my Love.

Ofwa. Even Love's an Empire too; The Noble Soul,
Like Kings, is Covetous of fingle Sway.

Arth. I blame ye not, for loving *Emmeline*:
But fince the Soul is free, and Love is choice,
You fhou'd have made a Conqueft of her
    Mind,
And not have forc'd her Perfon by a Rape.
  Ofwa. Whether by Force, or Stratagem,
    we gain;
Still Gaining is our End, in War or Love.
Her Mind's the Jewel, in her Body lock'd;
If I would gain the Gem, and want the Key,
It follows I muft feize the Cabinet:
But to fecure your fear, her Honour is
    untouch'd.
  Arth. Was Honour ever fafe in Brutal
    Hands?
So fafe are Lambs within the Lyons Paw;
Ungrip'd and plaid with, till fierce Hunger
    calls,
Then Nature shews it felf; the clofe-hid
    Nails
Are ftretch'd, and open'd, to the panting Prey.
But if indeed, you are fo Cold a Lover ——
  Ofwa. Not Cold, but Honourable.
  Arth. Then Reftore her.
That done, I shall believe you Honourable.
  Ofwa. Think'ft thou I will forego a Victor's
    Right?
  Arth. Say rather, of an Impious Ravisher.
That Caftle, were it wall'd with Adamant,

Can hide thy Head, but till to Morrow's
    Dawn.

  Oſwa. And e'er to Morrow, I may be a
    God,

If *Emmeline* be kind: But kind or cruel,

I tell thee, *Arthur*, but to ſee this Day,

That Heavenly Face, tho' not to have her
    mind,

I would give up a hundred Years of Life,

And bid Fate cut to Morrow.

  Arth. It ſoon will come, and thou repent
    too late;

Which to prevent, I'll bribe thee to be honeſt.

Thy Noble Head, accuſtom'd to a Crown,

Shall wear it ſtill: Nor ſhall thy hand forget

The Sceptre's uſe: From *Medway*'s pleaſing
    Stream,

To *Severn*'s Roar, be thine.

In ſhort, Reſtore my Love, and ſhare my
    Kingdom.

  Oſw. Not, tho' you ſpread my Sway from
    Thames to *Tyber*;

Such Gifts might bribe a King, but not
    a Lover.

  Arth. Then prithee give me back my
    Kingly Word,

Paſs'd for thy ſafe return; and let this Hour,

In ſingle Combate, Hand to Hand, decide

The Fate of Empire, and of *Emmeline*.

Ofwa. Not, that I fear, do I decline this
    Combat;
And not decline it neither, but defer:
When *Emmeline* has been my Prize as long
As she was thine, I dare thee to the Duel.
Arth. I nam'd your utmoſt Term of Life;
    To Morrow.
Ofwa. You are not Fate.
Arth. But Fate is in this Arm.
You might have made a Merit of your Theft.
Ofwa. Ha! Theft! Your Guards can tell,
    I ſtole her not.
Arth. Had I been preſent ——
Ofwa. Had you been preſent, she had been
    mine more Nobly.
Arth. There lies your way.
Ofwa. My way lies where I pleaſe.
Expect (for *Ofwald*'s Magick cannot fail)
A long to Morrow, e'er your Arms prevail;
Or if I fall, make Room ye bleſt above,
For one who was undone, and dy'd for Love.
              [*Exit* Ofwald *and his Party.*
Arth. There may be one black Minute e'er
    to Morrow:
For who can tell, what Pow'r, and Luſt,
    and Charms,
May do this Night? To Arms, with ſpeed,
    to Arms,   [*Exit.*

ACT III.

Enter Arthur, Conon *and* Aurelius.

Con. Furle up our Colours, and Unbrace
  our Drums;
Dislodge betimes; and quit this fatal Coaſt.
  Arth. Have we forgot to Conquer?
  Aur. Caſt off hope:
Th' Imbattl'd Legions of Fire, Air, and Earth,
Are banded for our Foes.
For going to diſcover, with the Dawn,
Yon Southern Hill, which promis'd to the
  Sight
A Rife more eaſie to attack the Fort,
Scarce had we ſtept on the Forbidden
  Ground,
When the Woods shook, the Trees ſtood
  briſtling up;
A Living Trembling Nodded through the
  Leaves.
  Arth. Poplars, and Aſpen-Boughs, a Pan-
  nick Fright.
  Con. We thought ſo too, and doubled ſtill
  our pace.
But ſtrait a rumbling Sound, like bellowing
  Winds,
Roſe and grew loud; Confus'd with Howls
  of Wolves,

And Grunts of Bears; and dreadful Hiſs
    of Snakes;
Shrieks more than Humane; Globes of
    Hail pour'd down
An Armed Winter, and Inverted Day.
  Arth. Dreadful, indeed!
  Aur. Count then our Labour's loſt:
For other way lies none, to mount the Cliff,
Unleſs we borrow Wings, and ſail through Air.
  Arth. Now I perceive a Danger worthy me.
'Tis *Oſmond*'s work, a band of Hell-hir'd Slaves:
Be mine the hazard, mine shall be the Fame.
    [Arthur *is going out, but is met by* Merlin, *who*
     takes him by the Hand, and brings him back.

Enter Merlin.

  Mer. Hold, Sir, and wait Heav'ns time;
    th' Attempt's too dangerous.
There's not a Tree in that Inchanted Grove,
But numbred out, and given by tale
    to Fiends;
And under every Leaf a Spirit couch'd.
But by what method to diſsolve theſe Charms,
Is yet unknown to me.
  Arth. Hadſt thou been here, (for what can
    thwart thy Skill?)
Nor *Emmeline* had been the boaſt of *Oſwald*;
Nor I, fore-warn'd, been wanting to her
    Guard.

5

Con. Her darkn'd Eyes had feen the Light
    of Heav'n;
That was thy promife too, and this the
    time.
Mer. Nor has my Aid been abfent, tho'
    unfeen,
With Friendly Guides in your benighted Maze:
Nor *Emmeline* shall longer want the Sun.
Arth. Is there an end of Woes?
Mer. There is, and fudden.
I have employ'd a fubtil Airy Spright
T' explore the paffage, and prepare my way.
My felf, mean time, will view the Magick
    Wood,
To learn whereon depends its Force.
Con. But *Emmeline* ——
Mer. Fear not: This Vial shall reftore
    her fight.
Arth. Oh might I hope (and what's
    impoffible
To *Merlin*'s Art) to be my felf the bearer,
That with the Light of Heav'n she may
    difcern
Her Lover firft.
Mer. 'Tis wondrous hazardous;
Yet I forefee th' Event, 'tis fortunate.
I'll bear ye fafe, and bring ye back unharm'd:
Then lofe not precious Time, but follow me.
        [*Exeunt Omnes*, Merlin *leading* Arthur.

Enter Philidel. *Scene, a Deep Wood.*

Phil. I left all fafe behind;
For in the hindmoſt quarter of the Wood,
My former Lord, Grim *Oſmond*, walks the
    Round:
Calls o'er the Names, and Schools the tardy
    Sprights.
His Abſence gives me more ſecurity.
At every Walk I paſs'd, I drew a Spell.
So that if any Fiend, abhorring Heav'n,
There ſets his Foot, it roots him to the
    Ground.
Now cou'd I but diſcover *Emmeline*,
My Task were fairly done.
    [*Walking about, and Prying betwixt the Trees.*

Enter Grimbald *rushing out: He ſeizes* Philidel,
    and binds him in a Chain.

Grimb. O Rebel, have I caught thee!
Phil. Ah me! What hard mishap!
Grimb. What juſt Revenge!
Thou miſcreant Elf, thou Renegado Scout,
So clean, ſo furbish'd, ſo renew'd in White,
The Livery of our Foes; I ſee thee through:
What mak'ſt thou here? Thou trim Apoſtate,
    ſpeak.
Thou shak'ſt for fear, I feel thy falſe Heart
    Pant.

Phil. Ah mighty *Grimbald*,
Who would not Fear, when ſeiz'd in thy
    ſtrong Gripes;
But hear me, Oh Renown'd, Oh worthy Fiend,
The Favourite of our Chief.
  Grimb. Away with fulſome Flattery,
The Food of Fools; thou know'ſt where laſt
    we met,
When but for thee, the Chriſtians had been
    ſwallow'd
In quaking Bogs, and Living ſent to Hell.
  Phil. Aye, then I was ſeduc'd by *Merlin*'s
    Art,
And half perſuaded by his ſoothing Tales,
To hope for Heav'n; as if Eternal Doom
Cou'd be Revers'd, and undecreed for me:
But I am now ſet Right.
  Grimb. Oh ſtill thou think'ſt to fly a Fool
    to Mark.
  Phil. I fled from *Merlin*, free as Air that
    bore me,
T' unfold to *Oſmond* all his deep Deſigns.
  Grimb. I believe nothing, Oh thou fond
    Impoſtor,
When wert thou laſt in Hell? Is not thy
    Name
Forgot, and Blotted from th' Infernal Roll?
But ſince thou ſay'ſt, thy Errand was
    to *Oſmond*,

To *Ofmond* shalt thou go; March, know thy
    Driver.

  Phil. Kneeling.] Oh fpare me, *Grimbald,* and
    I'll be thy Slave:

Tempt Hermits for thee, in their Holy Cells,
And Virgins in their Dreams.

  Grimb. Canft thou, a Devil, hope to cheat
    a Devil?

A Spy; why that's a Name abhorr'd in Hell;
Hafte forward, forward, or I'll Goad thee on,
With Iron Spurs.

  Phil. But ufe me kindly then:

Pull not fo hard to hurt my Airy Limbs;
I'll follow thee unforc'd; look, there's thy way.

  Grimb. Ay there's the way indeed; but for
    more furety

I'll keep an Eye behind: Not one word more,
But follow decently.

      [Grimbald *goes out, dragging* Philidel.

  Phil. afide.] So catch him Spell.

  Grimb. Within.] Oh help me, help me, *Philidel.*

  Phil. Why, What's the matter?

  Grimb. Oh, I am infnar'd:

Heav'ns Birdlime wraps me round, and glues
    my Wings.

Loofe me, and I will free thee;
Do, and I'll be thy Slave.

  Phil. What, to a Spy, a Name abhorr'd
    in Hell?

Grimb. Do not infult, Oh, Oh, I grow
    to Ground;
The Fiery Net draws clofer on my Limbs.
  Phil. Thou shalt not have the Eafe to
    curfe in Torments:
Be Dumb for one half hour; fo long my
    Charm
Can keep thee Silent, and there lie
Till *Ofmond* breaks thy Chain.
              [Philidel *unbinds his own Fetters.*

       Enter to him Merlin, *with a Vial in*
           his Hand; and Arthur.

  Mer. Well haft thou wrought thy Safety
    with thy Wit,
My *Philidel*; go Meritorious on.
Me, other Work requires, to view the Wood,
And learn to make the dire inchantments void.
Mean time attend King *Arthur* in my Room;
Shew him his Love, and with thefe
    Soveraign Drops
Reftore her fight.
         [*Exit* Merlin *giving a Vial to* Philidel.
  Phil. **We muft work, we muft haft;*
     Noon-Tyde Hour is almoft paft:
     Sprights, that glimmer in the Sun,
     Into Shades already run..
     Ofmond *will be here anon.**

    * No setting of this lyric has survived.

Enter Emmeline *and* Matilda, *at the far
end of the Wood.*

Arth. O yonder, yonder she's already found:
My Soul directs my fight, and flies before it.
Now, Gentle Spirit, ufe thy utmoft Art;
Unfeal her Eyes; and this way lead her Steps.
                    [Arthur *withdraws behind the Scene.*
[Emmeline *and* Matilda *come forward to the
Front.*
[Philidel *approaches* Emmeline, *fprinkling fome
of the Water over her Eyes, out of the Vial.*
Phil.   *Thus, Thus I infufe
            Thefe Soveraign Dews.
            Fly back, ye Films, that Cloud her fight,
            And you, ye Chryftal Humours bright,
            Your Noxious Vapours purg'd away,
            Recover, and admit the Day,
            Now caft your Eyes abroad, and fee
                All but me.*

Em. Ha! What was that? Who fpoke?
Mat. I heard the Voice; 'tis one of *Ofmond*'s
        Fiends.
Em. Some bleffed Angel fure; I feel my Eyes
Unfeal'd, they walk abroad, and a new World
Comes rushing on, and ftands all gay before me.
Mat. Oh Heavens! Oh Joy of Joys! she has
        her fight!

        * No setting of this lyric has survived.

Em. I am new-born; I shall run mad for
    Pleasure.   [*Staring on* Mat.
Are Women fuch as thou? Such Glorious
    Creatures?
Arth. afide.] Oh how I envy her, to be
    firft feen!
Em. Stand farther; let me take my fill
    of Sight.   [*Looking up.*
What's that above, that weakens my new
    Eyes,
Makes me not fee, by feeing?
Mat. 'Tis the Sun.
Em. The Sun, 'tis fure a God, if that
    be Heav'n:
Oh, if thou art a Creature, beft and faireft,
How well art thou, from Mortals fo remote,
To shine, and not to burn, by near approach!
How haft thou light'ned even my very
    Soul,
And let in Knowledge by another fenfe!
I gaze about, new-born, to Day and thee;
A Stranger yet, an Infant of the World!
Art thou not pleas'd, *Matilda*? Why, like me,
Doft thou not look and wonder?
Mat. For thefe Sights
Are to my Eyes familiar.
Em. That's my joy.
Not to have feen before: For Nature now
Comes all at once, confounding my Delight.

But ah! what thing am I? Fain wou'd
　　I know;
Or am I blind, or do I fee but half?
With all my Care, and, looking round about,
I cannot view my Face.

　Mat. None fee themfelves,
But by reflection; in this Glafs you may.
　　　　　　　　　　[*Gives her a Glafs.*

　Em. taking ⌠ What's this?
the Glafs, and ⟨ It holds a Face within it: Oh
looking. ⌡ 　fweet Face;
It draws the Mouth, and
Smiles, and looks upon me;
And talks; but yet I cannot hear it Speak:
The pretty thing is Dumb.

　Mat. The pretty thing
You fee within the Glafs, is you.

　Em. What, am I two? Is this another me?
Indeed it wears my Cloaths, has Hands
　　like mine;
And Mocks what e're I do; but that I'm fure
I am a Maid, I'd fwear it were my Child.
　　　　　　　　　　[Matilda *looks.*
Look, my *Matilda*; We both are in the Glafs,
Oh, now I know it plain; they are our Names
That peep upon us there.

　Mat. Our Shadows, Madam.

　Em. Mine is a prettier Shadow far, than
　　thine.

6

I Love it; let me Kiſs my t'other Self.

[Kiſſing the Glaſs, and hugging it.

Alas I've kiſs'd it Dead; the fine Thing's gone;
Indeed it Kiſs'd ſo Cold, as if 'twere Dying.

[Arthur *comes forward ſoftly; ſhewing
himſelf behind her.*

'Tis here again.

Oh no, this Face is neither mine nor thine;
I think the Glaſs has Born another Child.

[She turns and ſees Arthur.

Ha! What art thou, with a new kind of Face,
And other Cloaths, a Noble Creature too;
But taller, bigger, fiercer in thy Look;
Of a Comptrolling Eye, Majeſtick make?

Mat. Do you not know him, Madam?

Em. Is't a Man?

Arth. Yes, and the moſt unhappy of my
Kind,

If you have chang'd your Love.

Em. My deareſt Lord!

Was my Soul blind; and cou'd not that look
out,

To know you e're you Spoke? Oh Counter-
part

Of our ſoft Sex; Well are ye made our Lords;
So bold, ſo great, ſo God-like are ye form'd.
How can ye Love ſuch ſilly Things as Women?

Arth. Beauty like yours commands: and
Man was made

But a more boifterous, and a ftronger Slave,
To you, the beft Delights of human Kind.
   Em. But are ye mine? is there an end
      of War?
Are all thofe Trumpets Dead themfelves,
    at laft,
That us'd to kill Men with their Thundring
    Sounds?
   Arth. The Sum of War is undecided yet:
And many a breathing Body muft be Cold,
E're you are free.
   Em. How came ye hither then?
   Arth. By *Merlin*'s Art, to fnatch a short-
    liv'd Blifs:
To feed my Famish'd Love upon your Eyes
One Moment, and depart.
   Em. O moment, worth ——
Whole Ages paft, and all that are to come!
Let Love-fick *Ofwald*, now unpitied mourn;
Let *Ofmond* mutter Charms to Sprights in
    vain,
To make me Love him; all shall not change
   my Soul.
   Arth. Ha! Does the Inchanter practice Hell
   upon you?
Is he my Rival too?
   Em. Yes, but I hate him;
For when he fpoke, through my shut Eyes
    I faw him;

His Voice look'd ugly, and breath'd brim-
 ſtone on me:
And then I firſt was glad that I was blind,
Not to behold Damnation.
 [*Phil.* This time is left me to Congratu-
 late
Your new-born Eyes; and tell you what
 you gain
By ſight reſtor'd, and viewing him you
 love.
Appear, you Airy Forms:
     [*Airy Spirits appear in the Shapes*
       of Men and Women.
Man ſings. **O Sight, the Mother of Deſires,*
    What Charming Objects doſt thou yield!
     'Tis ſweet, when tedious Night
      expires,
    To ſee the Roſie Morning gild
     The Mountain Tops, and paint
     the Field!
    But, when Clorinda *comes in ſight,*
    She makes the Summers Day more
     bright;
    And when she goes away, 'tis Night.
 Chor. *When Fair* Clorinda *comes in*
    ſight, &c.
Wom. ſings. *'Tis ſweet the Blushing Morn to*
    view;
    And Plains adorn'd with Pearly Dew:
   * No setting of this has survived.

　　　　But such cheap Delights to see,
　　　　　Heaven and Nature,
　　　　　Give each Creature;
　　　　They have Eyes, as well as we.
　　　This is the Joy, all Joys above
　　　　　To see, to see,
　　　　　That only she,
　　　That only she we love!

Chor.　　*This is the Joy, all Joys above,* &c.
Man sings.　*And, if we may discover,*
　　　　What Charms both Nymph and Lover,
　　　　'Tis, when the Fair at Mercy lies,
　　　With Kind and Amorous Anguish,
　　　To Sigh, to Look, to Languish,
　　　On each others Eyes!

Chor. of all ⎫
Men and Wom.⎰ *And if we may discover,* &c.

Phil. Break off your musick; for our Foes
　　are near.　　　　　　　[*Spirits vanish.*]

Enter Merlin.

Merl. My Soveraign, we have hazarded
　　too far;
But Love excuses you, and prescience me.
Make haste; for *Osmond* is even now alarm'd,
And greedy of Revenge, is hasting home.

Arth. Oh take my Love with us, or leave
　　me here.

Merl. I cannot, for she's held by Charms
　　too strong:

Which, with the Inchanted Grove muſt
    be deſtroy'd;
Till when, my Art is vain: But fear not,
    Emmeline;
Th' Enchanter has no Pow'r on Innocence.
  Em. to Arth. Farewel, Since we muſt part:
    When you are gone,
I'll look into my Glaſs, juſt where you look'd;
To find your Face again;
If 'tis not there, I'll think on you ſo long,
My Heart ſhall make your Picture for my Eyes.
  Arth. Where-e'er I go, my Soul ſhall ſtay
    with thee:
'Tis but my Shadow that I take away;
True Love is never happy but by halves;
An *April* Sun-shine, that by fits appears,
It ſmiles by Moments, but it mourns by Years.
      [*Exeunt* Arthur *and* Merlin *at one Door.*

Enter Oſmond *at the other Door, who gazes on*
    Emmeline, *and she on him.*

  Em. *Matilda* ſave me, from this ugly Thing,
This Foe to ſight, Speak, doſt thou know
    him?
  Matil. Too well; 'tis *Oſwald*'s Friend, the
    great Magician.
  Em. It cannot be a Man, he's ſo unlike the
    Man I Love.
  Oſm. aſide. Death to my Eyes, she ſees!

Em. I wish I cou'd not; but I'll clofe
    my Sight,
And shut out all I can —— It wo'not be;
Winking, I fee thee ftill, thy odious Image
Stares full into my Soul; and there infects
    the Room
My *Arthur* shou'd poffefs.
   Ofm. afide. I find too late,
That *Merlin* and her Lover have been here.
If I was fir'd before, when she was Blind,
Her Eyes dart Lightning now, she muft
    be mine.
   Em. I prithee Dreadful Thing, tell me thy
    Bufinefs here;
And if thou canft, Reform that odious Face;
Look not fo Grim upon me.
   Ofm. My Name is *Ofmond*, and my Bufinefs
    Love.
   Em. Thou haft a grizly look; forbidding
    what thou ask'ft,
If I durft tell thee fo.
   Ofm. My Pent-Houfe Eye-Brows, and my
    Shaggy Beard
Offend your Sight, but thefe are Manly Signs;
Faint White and Red, abufe your
    Expectations;
Be Woman; know your Sex, and Love full
    Pleafures.
   Em. Love from a Monfter, Fiend!

Ofm. Come you muſt Love, or you muſt
 ſuffer Love;
No Coineſs, None, for I am Maſter here.
 Em. And when did *Ofwald* give away his
 Power,
That thou preſum'ſt to Rule? Be ſure I'll
 tell him:
For as I am his Priſoner, he is mine.
 Ofm. Why then thou art a Captive to
 a Captive.
O'er labour'd with the Fight, oppreſt with
 Thirſt:
That *Ofwald* whom you mention'd call'd
 for Drink:
I mix'd a Sleepy Potion in his Bowl;
Which he and his Fool Friend, quaff'd greedily,
The happy Doſe wrought the deſir'd effect;
Then to a Dungeon's depth, I ſent both Bound:
Where ſtow'd with Snakes and Adders now
 they lodge;
Two Planks their Beds; Slippery with Ooſe
 and Slime:
The Rats brush o'er their Faces with their
 Tails;
And croaking Paddocks crawl upon their
 Limbs.
Since when the Garriſon depends on me;
Now know you are my Slave.
 Mat. He ſtrikes a Horror through my Blood.

Em. I Freeze, as if his impious Art had fix'd
My Feet to Earth.

Ofm. But Love shall thaw ye.
I'll show his force in Countries cak'd with Ice,
Where the pale Pole-Star in the North of
    Heav'n
Sits high, and on the frory Winter broods;
Yet there Love Reigns: For proof, this
    Magick Wand
Shall change the Mildnefs of fweet *Britains*
    Clime
To *Yzeland* and the fartheft *Thule*'s Froft;
Where the Proud God, difdaining Winters
    Bounds,
O'er-leaps the Fences of Eternal Snow,
And with his Warmth, fupplies the diftant Sun.

    [Ofmond *ftrikes the Ground with his Wand:*
    The Scene changes to a Profpect of Winter in
    Frozen Countries.

Cupid *Defcends.*

Cup. fings.   *What ho, thou* Genius *of the Clime,*
             what ho!
             Ly'ft thou asleep beneath thofe Hills
             of Snow?
             Stretch out thy Lazy Limbs; awake,
             awake,
             And Winter from thy Furry Mantle
             shake.

Genius *Arifes*

Genius.   *What Power art thou, who from below,*
          Haft made me Rife, unwillingly, and
              slow,
          From Beds of Everlafting Snow!
          See'ft thou not how ftiff, and wondrous
              old,
          Far unfit to bear the bitter Cold,
          I can fcarcely move, or draw my Breath;
          Let me, let me, Freeze again to Death.

Cupid.   *Thou Doting Fool forbear, forbear;*
          What, Doft thou Dream of Freezing here?
          At Loves appearing, all the Skie
              clearing.
           The Stormy Winds their Fury fpare:
          Winter fubduing and Spring renewing,
            My Beams create a more Glorious
              Year,
          Thou Doting Fool, forbear, forbear;
          What, Doft thou Dream of Freezing
              here?

Genius.   *Great Love, I know thee now;*
          Eldeft of the Gods art Thou:
          Heav'n and Earth, by Thee were made.
           Humane Nature,
           Is thy Creature,
          Every Where Thou art obey'd.

Cupid.   *No part of my Dominion shall be waste,*
   To spread my Sway, and Sing my
      Praise,
   Ev'n here I will a People raise,
   Of kind embracing Lovers, and
     embraced.

(Cupid waves his Wand upon which the
 Scene opens, and discovers a Prospect of
 Ice and Snow to the end of the Stage.

 [Singers and Dancers, Men and Women,
      appear.

Man.*   *See, see, we assemble,*
   Thy Revels to hold:
   Though quiv'ring with Cold,
   We Chatter and Tremble.†
Cupid.   *'Tis I, 'tis I, 'tis I, that have warm'd ye;*
   In spight of Cold Weather,
   I've brought ye together:
   'Tis I, 'tis I, 'tis I, that have
     arm'd ye.
Chor.   *'Tis Love, 'tis Love, 'tis Love that has*
     warm'd us.
   In spight of Cold Weather,
   He brought us together:
  'Tis Love, 'tis Love, 'tis Love that has
     arm'd us.

   * Set by Purcell as a chorus.
   † Purcell adds a dance here.

Cupid.* *Sound a Parley, ye Fair, and surrender;*
        Set your selves, and your Lovers at ease;
        He's a Grateful Offender
        Who Pleasure dare seize:
        But the Whining pretender
        Is sure to displease.

                        2.

        Since the Fruit of Desire is possessing
            'Tis Unmanly to Sigh and Complain;
        When we Kneel for Redressing,
            We move your Disdain:
        Love was made for a Blessing,
            And not for a Pain.†
                [A Dance; after which the Singers
                        and Dancers depart.

  Em. I cou'd be pleas'd with any one but thee,
Who entertain my fight with such Gay Shows,
As Men and Women moving here and there;
That coursing one another in their Steps,
Have made their Feet a Tune.
  Osmo. What, Coying it again!
No more; but make me happy to my Gust,
That is, without your struggling.
  Em. From my fight,
Thou all thy Devils in one, thou dar'st not
        force me.

  * Set by Purcell as a duet for Cupid and the Genius.
  † Purcell repeats the chorus "'Tis Love."

Ofmo. You teach me well, I find you wou'd
  be Ravish'd;
I'll give you that excufe your Sex defires.
> [*He begins to lay hold on her,
> and they ftruggle.*

Grimb. Within.] O help me, Mafter, help
  me!

Ofmo. Who's that, my *Grimbald*! Come and
  help thou me:
For 'tis thy work t' affift a Ravisher.

Grimb. Within.] I cannot ftir; I am fpell
  caught by *Philidel*,
And purs'd within a Net. With a huge heavy
  weight of holy Words,
Laid on my Head that keeps me down from
  rifing.

Ofmo. I'll read 'em backwards, and releafe
  thy Bonds:
Mean time go in ——   [*To* Emmeline.
Prepare your felf, and eafe my Drudgery:
But if you will not fairly be enjoy'd,
A little honeft Force, is well employ'd.
> [*Exit* Ofmond.

Em. Heav'n be my Guard, I have no
  other Friend!
Heav'n ever prefent to thy fuppliants Aid,
Protect and pity Innocence betray'd.
> [*Exeunt* Emmeline *and* Matilda.

Enter Ofmond, *Solus.*

Now I am fetl'd in my Force-full Sway;
Why then, I'll be Luxurious in my Love;
Take my full Guft, and fetting Forms afide,
I'll bid the Slave, that fires my Blood, lie
    down.   [*Seems to be going off.*

Enter Grimbald, *who meets him.*

Grimb. Not fo faft, Mafter, Danger
    threatens thee:
There's a black Cloud defcending from above,
Full of Heav'ns Venom, burfting o'er thy
    Head.
  Ofmo. Malicious Fiend, thou ly'ft: For I
    am fenc'd
By Millions of thy Fellows, in my Grove:
I bad thee, when I freed thee from the Charm,
Run fcouting through the Wood, from Tree
    to Tree,
And look if all my Devils were on Duty:
Hadft thou perform'd thy Charge, thou
    tardy Spright,
Thou wouldft have known no Danger
    threatn'd me.
  Grim. When did a Devil fail in Diligence?
Poor Mortal, thou thy felf art overfeen;

I have been there, and thence I bring this
    News.
Thy fatal Foe, great *Arthur*, is at hand;
Merlin has ta'en his time while thou wert
    abfent,
T' obferve thy Charaêters, their Force, and
    Nature,
And Counterwork thy Spells.
  Ofmo. The Devil take *Merlin*;
I'll caft 'em all anew, and inftantly,
All of another Mould; be thou at hand.
Their Compofition was, before, of Horror;
Now they fhall be of Blandifhment, and Love;
Seducing Hopes, foft Pity, tender Moans:
Art fhall meet Art; and, when they think
    to win,
The Fools fhall find their Labour to begin.
           [*Exeunt* Ofmo. *and* Grimb.

   Enter Arthur, *and* Merlin *at another Door.*

    Scene of the Wood continues.

  Mer. Thus far it is permitted me to go;
But all beyond this Spot, is fenc'd with
    Charms;
I may no more; but only with advice.
  Arth. My Sword fhall do the reft.
  Mer. Remember well, that all is but
    Illufion;
Go on; good Stars attend thee.

Arth. Doubt me not.

Mer. Yet in prevention

Of what may come, I'll leave my *Philidel*

To watch thy Steps, and with him leave
    my Wand;

The touch of which, no Earthy Fiend can
    bear,

In what e'er Shape transform'd, but muſt
    lay down

His borrow'd Figure, and confeſs the Devil.

Once more Farewel, and Proſper.

                           [*Exit* Merlin.

  Arth. Walking.] No Danger yet, I ſee no
    walls of Fire,

No City of the Fiends, with Forms obſcene,

To grin from far, on Flaming Battlements.

This is indeed the Grove I ſhou'd deſtroy;

But where's the Horrour? Sure the Prophet
    err'd.

Hark! Muſick, and the warbling Notes of
    Birds;   [*Soft Muſick.**

Hell entertains me, like ſome welcome Gueſt.

More Wonders yet; yet all delightful too,

A Silver Current to forbid my paſſage,

And yet to invite me, ſtands a Golden Bridge:

Perhaps a Trap, for my Unwary Feet

  * In the absence of any music from the *King Arthur*
score suitable at this moment a Rondeau from Purcell's
music to *The Gordian Knot Untied* was inserted for the
1928 production.

To fink, and Whelm me underneath the Waves;
With Fire or Water, let him wage his War,
Or all the Elements at once; I'll on.

> [*As he is going to the Bridge, two Syrens arife from the Water; They shew themfelves to the Wafte, and Sing.*

[1 Syren.   *O pafs not on, but ftay,*
       And wafte the Joyous Day
       With us in gentle Play:
      Unbend to Love, unbend thee:
       O lay thy Sword afide,
       And other Arms provide;
      For other Wars attend thee,
       And fweeter to be try'd.

Chor.   *For other Wars, &c.*]

Both Sing. *Two Daughters of this Aged Stream*
        are we;
      And both our Sea-green Locks have
        comb'd for thee;
      Come Bath with us an Hour or two,
      Come Naked in, for we are fo;
      What Danger from a Naked Foe?
      Come Bath with us, come Bath,
        and share,
      What Pleafures in the Floods appear;
      We'll beat the Waters till they bound,
      And Circle round, around, around,
       And Circle round, around.

   * No setting of this has survived.

8

Arth. A Lazie Pleafure trickles through my
    Veins;
Here could I ftay, and well be Cozen'd here.
But Honour calls; Is Honour in fuch hafte?
Can he not Bait at fuch a pleafing Inn?
No; for the more I look, the more I long;
Farewel, ye Fair Illufions, I muft leave ye.
While I have Power to fay, that I muft leave ye.
Farewel, with half my Soul I ftagger off;
How dear this flying Victory has coft,
When, if I ftay to ftruggle, I am loft.

    [*As he is going forward,* Nymphs *and* Sylvans
      come out from behind the Trees, Bafe and two
      Trebles fing the following Song *to a* Minuet.

    [Dance with the Song, all with Branches
        in their Hands.

I.

Song.* *How happy the Lover,*
      How eafie his Chain,
      How pleafing his Pain?
      How fweet to difcover!
      He fighs not in vain.*
    †*For Love every Creature*
    Is form'd by his Nature;
    No Joys are above
    The Pleafures of Love.†

[The Dance continues with the fame Meafure
        play'd alone.

* Repeated in chorus.   † Set as a duet and chorus.

II.

In vain are our Graces,
   In vain are your Eyes,
   If Love you defpife;
  When Age furrows Faces,
   *'Tis time to be wife.**
 † *Then ufe the short Bleffing:*
   That Flies in Poffeffing:
   No Joys are above
   The Pleafures of Love.†

Arth. And what are thefe Fantaftick Fairy
   Joys,
To Love like mine? Falfe Joys, falfe
   Welcomes all,
Begone, ye *Sylvan* Trippers of the Green;
Fly after Night, and overtake the Moon.
   [*Here the Dancers, Singers and Syrens vanish.*
This goodly Tree feems Queen of all the
   Grove.
The Ringlets round her Trunk declare her
   guilty
Of many Midnight-Sabbaths Revell'd here.
Her will I firft attempt.
   [Arthur *ftrikes at the Tree, and cuts it; Blood*
   fpouts out of it, a Groan follows, then a Shreik.
Good Heav'ns, what Monftrous Prodigies
   are thefe!

   * Set as a trio for three Nymphs.
   † Set as a trio for three Sylvans and Chorus.

Blood follows from my blow; the Wounded
    Rind

Spouts on my Sword, and Sanguine dies the
    Plain.

> [*He strikes again: A Voice of* Emmeline
> *from behind.*

  Em. from behind.] Forbear, if thou haft Pity,
    ah forbear!

Thefe Groans proceed not from a Sencelefs
    Plant,

No Spouts of Blood run welling from a Tree.
  Arth. Speak what thou art; I charge thee
    fpeak thy Being;

Thou that haft made my curdl'd Blood run
    back,

My Heart heave up; my Hair to rife in
    Briftles,

And fcarcely left a Voice to ask thy Name.
> [Emmeline *breaks out of the Tree,*
> *shewing her Arm Bloody.*

  Em. Whom thou haft hurt, Unkind and
    Cruel, fee;

Look on this Blood, 'tis fatal, ftill, to me

To bear thy Wounds, my Heart has felt 'em
    firft.

  Arth. 'Tis she; Amazement roots me to the
    Ground!

  Em. By cruel Charms, dragg'd from my
    peaceful Bower,

Fierce *Ofmond* clos'd me in this bleeding Bark;
And bid me ftand expos'd to the bleak Winds,
And Winter Storms; and Heav'ns
  Inclemency,
Bound to the Fate of this Hell-haunted Grove;
So that whatever Sword, or founding Axe,
Shall violate this Plant, muft pierce my Flesh,
And when that falls, I die ——
 Arth. If this be true,
O never, never, to be ended Charm,
At leaft by me; yet all may be illufion.
Break up, ye thickning Foggs, and filmy
  Mifts,
All that be-lye my Sight, and cheat my Senfe.
For Reafon ftill pronounces, 'tis not she,
And thus refolv'd ——
   [*Lifts up his Sword, as going to ftrike.*
 Em. Do, ftrike, *Barbarian*, ftrike;
And ftrew my mangled Limbs, with every
  ftroke,
Wound me, and double Kill me, with
  Unkindnefs,
That by thy Hand I fell.
 Arth. What shall I do, ye Powers?
 Em. Lay down thy Vengeful Sword; 'tis
  fatal here:
What need of `Arms, where no Defence
  is made?
A Love Sick Virgin, panting with Defire,

No Conscious Eye t' intrude on our Delights:
For this thou haft the *Syren's* Songs defpis'd;
For this, thy Faithful Paffion I Reward;
Hafte then, to take me longing to thy Arms.
   Arth. O Love! O *Merlin*! Whom should
     I believe?
   Em. Believe thy Self, thy Youth, thy Love,
     and me;
They only, they who pleafe themfelves, are
     Wife:
Difarm thy Hand, that mine may meet it bare.
   Arth. By thy leave, Reafon, here I throw
     thee off,
Thou load of Life: If thou wert made for
     Souls,
Then Souls shou'd have been made without
     their Bodies.
If, falling for the firft Created Fair,
Was *Adam*'s Fault, great Grandfire I forgive
     thee,
Eden was loft, as all thy Sons wou'd lofe it.
       [*Going towards* Emmeline, *and pulling
           off his Gantlet.*

Enter Philidel *running.*

   Phil. Hold, poor deluded Mortal, hold
     thy Hand;
Which if thou giv'ft, is plighted to a Fiend.
For proof, behold the Vertue of this Wand;

Th' Infernal Paint shall vanish from her Face,
And Hell shall ftand Reveal'd.
[*Strikes* Emmeline *with a Wand, who ftraight*
    defcends: Philidel *runs to the Defcent, and pulls*
    up Grimbald, *and binds him.*
Now fee to whofe Embraces thou wert falling.
Behold the Maiden Modefty of *Grimbald*,
The groffeft, earthieft, uglieft Fiend in Hell.
  Arth. Horror feizes me,
To think what Headlong Ruine I have
    tempted.
  Phil. Hafte to thy Work; a Noble ftroke
    or two
Ends all the Charms, and difenchants the
    Grove.
I'll hold thy Miftrefs bound.
  Arth. Then here's for Earneft;
        [*Strikes twice or thrice, and the Tree falls,*
         or finks: A Peal of Thunder immediately
         follows, with dreadful Howlings.
'Tis finifh'd, and the Dusk that yet remains,
Is but the Native Horrour of the Wood.
But I muft lofe no time; the Pafs is free;
Th' unroofted Fiends have quitted this
    Abode;
On yon proud Towers, before the day
    be done,
My glittering Banners shall be wav'd againft
    the fetting Sun.   [*Exit* Arth.

[*Phil.* Come on my furly Slave; come ftalk
        along,
And ftamp a mad-Man's pace, and drag
        thy Chain.
  Grim. I'll Champ and Foam upon't, till
        the blue Venom
Work upward to thy Hands, and loofe their
        hold.
  Phil. Know'ft thou this powerful Wand;
        'tis lifted up;
A fecond ftroke wou'd fend thee to the Centre,
Benumb'd and Dead, as far as Souls can Die.
  Grim. I wou'd thou wou'dft, to rid me of
        my Senfe:
I shall be whoop'd through Hell at my return,
Inglorious from the Mifchief I defign'd.
  Phil. And therefore fince thou loath'ft
        Ethereal Light,
The Morning Sun shall beat on thy black
        Brows;
The Breath thou draw'ft shall be of upper Air,
Hoftile to thee, and to thy Earthy make,
So light, fo thin, that thou sha't Starve,
        for want
Of thy grofs Food, till gafping thou shalt lie,
And blow it black, all Sooty to the Sky.
  [*Exit* Philidel, *dragging* Grimbald *after him.*]

Enter Ofmond *as Affrighted.*

Ofm. Grimbald made Prifoner, and my Grove
deftroy'd!
Now what can fave me —— Hark the Drums
and Trumpets!

           [Drums and Trumpets within.
Arthur is marching onward to the Fort,
I have but one Recourfe, and that's to
     Ofwald;
But will he Fight for me, whom I have
     injur'd?
No, not for me, but for himfelf he muft;
I'll urge him with the laft Neceffity;
Better give up my Miftrefs than my Life.
His force is much unequal to his Rival?
True; —— But I'll help him with my
     utmoft Art,
And try t' unravel Fate.   *[Exit* Ofmond.

Enter Arthur, Conon, Aurelius, Albanaĉt,
     and Soldiers.

Con. Now there remains but this one
     Labour more;
And if we have the Hearts of true Born
     Britains,
The forcing of that Caftle Crowns the Day.

Aur. The Works are weak, the Garrifon but
 thin,
Difpirited with frequent Overthrows,
Already wavering on their ill mann'd Walls.
 Alb. They shift their places oft, and fculk
 from War,
Sure Signs of pale Defpair, and eafie Rout;
It shews they place their Confidence in
  Magick,
And when their Devils fail, their Hearts
 are Dead.
 Arth. Then, where you fee 'em cluft'ring
 moft, in Motion,
And ftaggering in their Ranks, there prefs
 'em home;
For that's a Coward heap —— How's, this,
 a Sally?

  Enter Ofwald, Guillamar, *and Souldiers
   on the other fide.*

Beyond my Hopes, to meet 'em on the Square.
 Ofw. ad-⎫ Brave *Britains* hold; and thou
 vancing.⎭   their famous Chief
Attend what *Saxon Ofwald* will propofe.
He owns your Victory, but whether owing
To Valour, or to Fortune, that he doubts.
If *Arthur* dares afcribe it to the firft
And fingl'd from a Crowd, will tempt a
 Conqueft,

This *Ofwald* Offers, let our Troops retire,
And Hand to Hand, let us decide our Strife:
This if Refus'd, bear Witnefs Earth and
      Heaven,
Thou fteal'ft a Crown and Miftrefs
      undeferv'd.

  Arth. I'll not Ufurp thy Title of a Robber,
Nor will upbraid thee, that before I proffer'd
This fingle Combat, which thou didft avoid;
So glad I am, on any Terms to meet thee,
And not difcourage thy Repenting shame;
As once *Æneas* my Fam'd Anceftor,
Betwixt the *Trojan* and *Rutilian* Bands,
Fought for a Crown, and bright *Lavinia*'s
      Bed,
So will I meet thee, Hand to Hand oppos'd:
My Auguring Mind, affures the fame
      Succefs.

  To his Men. Hence out of view; If I am
      Slain, or yield,
Renounce me *Britains* for a Recreant Knight,
And let the *Saxon* peacefully enjoy
His former footing in our famous Isle.
To Ratifie thefe Terms, I fwear ——

  Ofw. You need not;
Your Honour is of Force, without your Oath.
I only add, that if I fall, or yeild,
Yours be the Crown, and *Emmeline*.

  Arth. That's two Crowns.

No more; we keep the looking Heav'ns and
    Sun
Too long in Expectation of our Arms.
            [*Both Armies go clear off the Stage.*

[*They Fight with Spunges in their Hands dipt in
    Blood; after some equal Passes and Closeing, they
    appear both Wounded:* Arthur *Stumbles among
    the Trees,* Ofwald *falls over him, they both
    Rise;* Arthur *Wounds him again, then* Ofwald
    Retreats. Enter Ofmond *from among the Trees,
    and with his Wand, strikes* Arthur's *Sword out
    of his Hand, and* Exit. Ofwald *pursues* Arthur.
    Merlin *enters, and gives* Arthur *his Sword, and*
    Exit; *they close, and* Arthur *in the fall Disarms*
    Ofwald.

Arth. Confeſs thy ſelf o'ercome, and ask
    thy Life.
Ofw. 'Tis not worth asking, when 'tis in
    thy Power.
Arth. Then take it as my Gift.
Ofw. A wretched Gift,
With loſs of Empire, Liberty, and Love.
        [[*A Confort of Trumpets within, proclaiming*
                Arthur's *Victory. While they Sound,*
                Arthur *and* Ofwald *ſeem to Confer.*
'Tis too much Bounty to a vanquish'd Foe;
Yet not enough to make me Fortunate.]
  Arth. Thy Life, thy Liberty, thy Honour Safe,

Lead back thy *Saxons* to their Ancient *Elbe*:
I wou'd Reftore thee fruitful *Kent*, the Gift
Of *Vortigern* for *Hengift*'s ill-brought aid,
But that my *Britains* brook no Foreign Power,
To Lord it in a Land, Sacred to Freedom;
And of its Rights Tenacious to the laft.
  Ofw. Nor more than thou haft offer'd
    wou'd I take.
I wou'd Refufe all *Britain*, held in Homage;
And own no other Mafters but the Gods.

Enter on one fide; Merlin, Emmeline, *and*
    Matilda. Conon, Aurelius, Albanaét, *with*
    British Soldiers, bearing King Arthur'*s Standard*
    difplay'd.
On the other fide; Guillamar *and* Ofmond, *with*
    Saxon Soldiers, dragging their Colours on the
    Ground.

	At length, at length, I have
Arth. *going to*	thee in my Arms;
Emm. *and em-*	Tho' our Malevolent Stars
bracing her.	have ftruggled hard,
	And held us long afunder.

  Em. We are fo fitted for each others Hearts,
That Heav'n had err'd, in making of a third,
To get betwixt, and intercept our Loves.
  Ofw. Were there but this, this only fight
    to fee,
The price of *Britain* shou'd not buy my ftay.

    Merl. Take hence that Monſter of
        Ingratitude,
Him, who betray'd his Maſter, bear him
        hence,
And in that loathſom Dungeon plunge him
        deep,
Where he plung'd Noble *Oſwald.*
    Oſm. That indeed is fitteſt for me,
For there I shall be near my Kindred
        Fiends,
And ſpare my *Grimbald*'s Pains to bear me
      to 'em.   [*Is carried off.*
    Mer. to Arth. For this Days Palm, and for
        thy former Aᶜts,
Thy *Britain* freed, and Foreign Force expell'd,
Thou, *Arthur,* haſt acquir'd a future Fame,
And of three Chriſtian Worthies, art the firſt:
And now at once, to treat thy Sight and Soul,
Behold what Rouling Ages shall produce:
The Wealth, the Loves, the Glories of our Isle,
Which yet like Golden-Oar, unripe in Beds,
Expeᶜt the Warm Indulgency of Heav'n
To call 'em forth to Light ——
    To *Oſw.* Nor thou, brave *Saxon* Prince
        diſdain our Triumphs;
Britains and *Saxons* shall be once one People;
One Common Tongue, one Common Faith
        shall bind
Our Jarring Bands, in a perpetual Peace.

[Merlin *waves his Wand; the Scene changes, and
  discovers the British Ocean in a Storm.* Æolus
  in a Cloud above: Four Winds hanging, &c.

Æolus   *Ye Blust'ring Brethren of the Skies,*
Singing.] *Whose Breath has ruffl'd all the
            Watry Plain,
          Retire, and let* Britannia *Rise
        In Triumph o'er the Main.
        Serene and Calm, and void of fear,
        The Queen of Islands must appear:
      *[*Serene and Calm, as when the Spring
        The New Created World began,
        And Birds on Boughs did softly sing,
        Their Peaceful Homage paid to Man,
        While* Eurus *did his Blasts forbear,
        In favour of the Tender Year.
        Retreat, Rude Winds, retreat
        To Hollow Rocks, your Stormy Seat;
        There swell your Lungs, and vainly,
            vainly threat.*]*

[*Æolus* ascends, and the four Winds fly off.
  The Scene opens, and discovers a calm Sea,
  to the end of the House. An *Island* arises,
  to a soft Tune; *Britannia* seated in the
  Island, with Fishermen at her Feet, &c. The
  Tune changes; the Fishermen come ashore,
  and dance a While; after which, *Pan* and
  a *Nereide* come on the Stage, and sing.

        * Omitted by Purcell.

Pan *and* Nereide *Sing.*

Round thy Coaſt, Fair Nymph of Britain,
   For thy Guard our Waters flow:
Proteus *all his Herd admitting,*
   On thy Greens to Graze below.
Foreign Lands thy Fishes Taſting,
*Learn from thee Luxurious Faſting.**

Song of three Parts.

For Folded Flocks, on Fruitful Plains,
The Shepherds and the Farmers Gains,
   Fair Britain *all the World outvies;*
And Pan, *as in* Arcadia *Reigns,*
   Where Pleaſure mixt with Profit lies.

2.

Though Jaſons *Office was Fam'd of old,*
The British *Wool is growing Gold;*
   No Mines can more of Wealth ſupply:
It keeps the Peaſant from the Cold,
   And takes for Kings the Tyrian *Dye.*

The laſt *Stanza* ſung over again betwixt *Pan*
and the *Nereide.* After which the former
Dance is varied, and goes on.

Enter Comus *with three Peaſants, who ſing the*
following SONG in Parts.

Com.   *Your Hay it is Mow'd and your Corn*
       is Reap'd;
      Your Barns will be full, and your
      Hovels heap'd:

* Repeated in chorus.

Come, my Boys, come;
Come, my Boys, come;
And merrily Roar out Harveſt Home;
Harveſt Home,
Harveſt Home;
And merrily Roar out Harveſt Home.

Chorus. *Come, my Boys, come,* &c.

1 Man. *We ha' cheated the Parſon, we'll cheat*
him agen;
For why ſhou'd a Blockhead ha' One in Ten?
One in Ten,
One in Ten;
For why ſhou'd a Blockhead ha' One in Ten?

Chorus. *One in Ten,*
One in Ten;
For why ſhou'd a Blockhead ha' One in Ten?

2. *For Prating ſo long like a Book-learn'd Sot,*
Till Pudding and Dumplin burn to Pot;
Burn to Pot,
Burn to Pot;
Till Pudding and Dumplin burn to Pot.

Chorus. *Burn to Pot,* &c.

3. *We'll toſs off our Ale till we canno' ſtand,*
And Hoigh for the Honour of Old England:
Old England,
Old England;
And Hoigh for the Honour of Old England.

Chorus. *Old* England, *&c.*

The Dance vary'd into a round Country-
Dance.

Enter Venus.

Venus. *Faireſt Isle, all Isles Excelling,*
    Seat of Pleaſures, and of Loves;
  Venus, here, will chuſe her Dwelling,
    And forſake her Cyprian Groves.

2.

Cupid from his Fav'rite Nation,
  Care and Envy will Remove;
Jealouſie, that poyſons Paſſion,
  And Deſpair that dies for Love.

3.

Gentle Murmurs, ſweet Complaining,
  Sighs that blow the Fire of Love;
Soft Repulſes, kind Diſdaining,
  Shall be all the Pains you prove.

4.

Every Swain shall pay his Duty,
  Grateful every Nymph shall prove;
And as theſe Excel in Beauty,
  Thoſe shall be Renown'd for Love;

[SONG by Mr *Howe*.*

She. *You ſay, 'Tis Love Creates the Pain,*
  Of which ſo ſadly you Complain;
  And yet wou'd fain Engage my Heart
  In that uneaſie cruel part:
  But how, Alas! think you, that I,
  Can bear the Wound of which you die?

* Omitted in the 1928 production solely on account of the length both of this Dialogue and of the whole scene.

2.

He.   *'Tis not my Paſſion makes my Care,*
         But your Indifference gives Deſpair:
         The Luſty Sun begets no Spring,
         Till Gentle Show'rs Aſſiſtance bring:
         So Love that Scorches, and Deſtroys,
         Till Kindneſs Aids, can cauſe no Joys.

3.

She. *Love has a Thouſand Ways to pleaſe,*
         But more to rob us of our Eaſe:
         For Wakeful Nights and Careful Days,
         Some Hours of Pleaſure he repays;
         But abſence ſoon, or Jealous Fears,
         O'erflow the Joys with Floods of Tears.

4.

He. †*By vain and ſenſeleſs Forms betray'd,*
         Harmleſs Love's th' Offender made;
         While we no other Pains endure,
         Than thoſe, that we our ſelves procure:
         But one ſoft Moment makes Amends
         For all the Torment that attends.

5.

Chorus of Both.

Let us love, let us love, and to Happineſs
         haſte;
Age and Wiſdom come too faſt:
Youth for Loving was deſign'd.

* Set by Purcell as a duet.   † Omitted by Purcell.

He alone. *I'll be conſtant, you be kind.*
She alone. *You be conſtant, I'll be kind.*
Both.   *Heav'n can give no greater Bleſſing.*
                Than faithful Love, and kind Poſſeſſing.]
[After the Dialogue, a Warlike Conſort: The
    Scene opens above, and diſcovers the Order
    of the Garter.

        Enter Honour, *Attended by* Hero's.

Merl. Theſe who laſt enter'd, are our
        Valiant *Britains,*
Who ſhall by Sea and Land Repel our Foes.
Now look above, and in Heav'ns High Abyſs,
Behold what Fame attends thoſe future
        Hero's.
Honour, who leads 'em to that Steepy Height,
In her Immortal Song, ſhall tell the reſt.

            (Honour ſings.)

                1.

Hon.   *St.* George, *the Patron of our Isle,*
            A Soldier, and a Saint,
            On that Auſpicious Order ſmile,
            Which Love and Arms will plant.

                2.

        Our Natives not alone appear
            To Court this Martial Prize;
            But Foreign Kings Adopted here,
            Their Crowns at home deſpiſe.

    * Purcell seems to have begun the Chorus here.

3.

Our Soveraign High, in Aweful State,
His Honours shall bestow;
And see his Scepter'd Subjects wait
On his Commands below.

[A full Chorus of the whole Song: After which
the Grand Dance.

Arth. to Merl. Wisely you have, whate'er
will please, reveal'd,
What wou'd displease, as wisely have
conceal'd:
Triumphs of War and Peace, at full ye show,
But swiftly turn the Pages of our Wo.
Rest we contented with our present State;
'Tis Anxious to enquire of future Fate;
That Race of Hero's is enough alone
For all unseen Disasters to atone.
Let us make haste betimes to Reap our share,
And not Resign them all the Praise of War.
But set th' Example; and their Souls Inflame,
To Copy out their Great Forefathers Fame.

THE EPILOGUE

Spoken by MRS BRACEGIRDLE

I'Ve had to Day a Dozen Billet-Doux
From Fops, and Wits, and Cits, and Bowftreet-
      Beaux;
Some from Whitehal, *but from the* Temple *more;*
A Covent Garden *Porter brought me four.*
I have not yet read all: But, without feigning,
We Maids *can make shrewd Guesses at your meaning.*
What if, to shew your Styles, I read 'em here?
Methinks I hear one cry, Oh Lord, forbear:
No, Madam, no; *by* Heav'n, that's too severe.
Well then, be safe ——
But swear henceforwards to renounce all Writing
And take this Solemn Oath of my Inditing,
As you love Eafe, and hate Campagnes and
      Fighting.
Yet, 'Faith, 'tis just to make some few Examples:
What if I shew'd you one or two for Samples?
Pulls one out.] *Here's one desires my Ladyship to*
      meet
At the kind Couch above in Bridges-Street.
Oh Sharping Knave! That wou'd have, you know what,
For a poor Sneaking Treat of Chocolat.
  Now, in the Name of Luck, I'll break this open,
Pulls out another.] *Because I Dreamt last Night*
      I had a Token;

The Superscription is exceeding pretty,
  To the Desire of all the Town and City.
  Now, Gallants, *you must know, this pretious* Fop,
Is Foreman of a Haberdashers-Shop:
One who devoutly Cheats; demure in Carriage;
And Courts me to the Holy Bands of Marriage.
But with a Civil Innuendo *too,*
My Overplus of Love shall be for you.
Reads.] Madam, I swear your Looks are so
    Divine,
When I set up, your Face shall be my Sign:
Tho Times are hard; to shew how I adore you,
Here's my whole Heart, and half a Guinea
    for you.
But have a care of *Beaux*; They're false, my
    Honey;
And which is worse, have not one Rag of Money.

  See how Maliciously the Rogue would wrong ye;
But I know better Things of some among ye.
My wisest way will be to keep the Stage,
And trust to the Good Nature of the Age;
And he that likes the Musick *and the* Play,
Shall be my Favourite Gallant to Day.]